FRANK LLOYD WRIGHT IN MONTANA

DARBY, STEVENSVILLE, AND WHITEFISH

Randall LeCocq

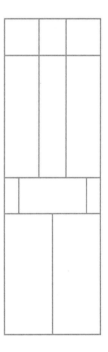

DRUMLUMMON
INSTITUTE

Helena, Montana

2013

FRANK LLOYD WRIGHT IN MONTANA
DARBY, STEVENSVILLE, AND WHITEFISH

Drumlummon *Montana Architecture Series*

Published by Drumlummon Institute, Helena, Montana.

Text © 2013 by Randall LeCocq

Front cover: *The Como Orchard Clubhouse shortly after construction. Photographer unknown. Courtesy of Montana Historical Society Photograph Archives.* **Back cover:** *Lockridge Clinic Building, currently Morrison and Frampton Law Firm, 2008, Whitefish, Montana. Courtesy of Jay Dooling..*

ISBN-10: 0976968452
ISBN-13: 978-0-9769684-5-0

Cataloging-in-Publication Data on file at the Library of Congress.

Drumlummon Institute is a 501(c)(3) nonprofit that seeks to foster a
deeper understanding of the rich culture(s) of Montana and the broader
American West through research, writing, and publishing.

Design: Geoff Wyatt, Wyatt Design, Helena, Montana

Manufactured in the United States of America.
10 9 8 7 6 5 4 3 2 1

DRUMLUMMON
INSTITUTE

710 Harrison Avenue • Helena, Montana 59601
www.drumlummon.org

ACKNOWLEDGMENTS

I would like to thank Rick Newby for editing and publishing this work through Drumlummon Institute, and for his friendship and constant guidance and encouragement in taking on this project highlighting Montana's Frank Lloyd Wright heritage. I would also like to thank Patty Dean, of the Montana Preservation Alliance, for sharing her expertise on architecture and the history of Montana's early twentieth-century development projects. I am grateful also for Patty's thorough review of this manuscript and for her suggestions. Kate Hampton of the Montana State Historic Preservation Office and the staff of the Montana Historical Society Photograph Archives provided wonderful photographs. I would also like to thank John Driscoll, who found new reference resources, took photographs, and helped me explore sites in the Bitterroot Valley, where he grew up. Tricia Smith and the staff of Art Resource in New York were very helpful and patient in providing photos from the Taliesin Archives and permission to use them. I offer special thanks to Charles Rowland, the owner of Alpine Meadows Ranch, and his staff, who were very helpful in guiding me on two occasions through the remaining Como Orchards cabins and offering assistance. I also thank the Moody family of Stevensville, Montana, for their memories and assistance in exploring the site of the former Bitter Root Inn. I would like to thank the Morrison-Frampton Law Firm in Whitefish for reviewing this transcript and for carefully preserving Frank Lloyd Wright's beautiful building as well as his memory. Finally, I want to thank the Taliesin Institute and Getty Research Institute for sharing materials and for preserving the memory of Frank Lloyd Wright.

FRANK LLOYD WRIGHT IN MONTANA
DARBY, STEVENSVILLE, AND WHITEFISH

Randall LeCocq

INTRODUCTION

On February 15, 1909, Frank Lloyd Wright arrived by train in Montana's Bitterroot Valley for a three-day stay that culminated in two major projects: a 1,600-acre "Como Orchard Summer Colony" near Darby, and a more ambitious "Bitter Root Town" near Stevensville. This was Wright's first commission in Montana. He was accompanied on the train by Chicago investors in the colony. Ultimately, fourteen buildings were built at the two sites, including two Prairie Style cabins that still exist near Darby and are visited by Wright enthusiasts and Bitterroot vacationers to this day. All the other buildings, including the larger centerpieces of the two projects, the Como Orchard Clubhouse and the Bitter Root Inn, have disappeared over time, but are important parts of Wright's legacy and Montana's history. There remains some mystery among Wright scholars about the failure to complete the overall projects and the degree of Wright's involvement in their execution, during a time of personal crisis for Wright.

The Bitterroot projects remain significant to architectural historians as early examples of architectural modernism, which was being developed simultaneously in Chicago and Europe in the first decade of the twentieth century, with Frank Lloyd Wright in the vanguard. They are models of Wright's early "Prairie House" designs, few of which are to be found outside of Wright's core midwestern U.S. homeland. The Bitterroot projects are also significant as early twentieth-century experiments in town planning, employing, in this case, Wright's idea of combining urban and agrarian lifestyles, providing a community close to nature, where like-minded families could live in "organic," uncluttered houses and cultivate their own ten-acre apple plots. Wright had dabbled in community planning prior to 1909, but the Bitterroot projects were his most ambitious schemes. Beyond their architectural significance, these projects are important pieces of Montana and U.S. history, associated with early twentieth-century railroad expansion, speculation, and general economic progress, mixed with a profusion of new ideas on communal living.[1]

Half a century later, in Whitefish, Montana, between Flathead Lake and Glacier National Park, Wright would create the Lockridge

Facing Page: Towering firs line the road to Alpine Meadows Ranch, formerly Como Orchard Summer Colony, Darby, Montana. Photograph by Kathryn Hampton. Courtesy of Montana State Historic Preservation Office.

Photograph of Lockridge Clinic Building, currently Morrison and Frampton Law Firm, 2008, Whitefish, Montana. Courtesy of Jay Dooling.

Photograph of Lockridge Clinic Building, currently Morrison and Frampton Law Firm, 2008, Whitefish, Montana. Courtesy of Jay Dooling.

Medical Clinic Building, now the Morrison and Frampton Law Firm. This office building would represent his last phase or modernist style, the "Usonian" buildings, which evolved gradually from his earlier "Prairie Style," "Textile Block," and Streamlined ("Fallingwater") phases. The Usonians are slicker than Wright's previous works, using more glass, concrete, plywood, and brick, and in a more geometric way. They are more modest buildings, with less intricate ornament such as art glass, resembling the postwar suburban ranch-style houses. But they still adhere to the same Wrightian architectural principles that he used in 1910 in the Bitterroot, combining form and function by eliminating added-on ornament and relying on uninterrupted flat planes and basic shapes. Design, again, would be provided by the building's geometry, engineering, and building materials. The building must have a natural feel through its use of brick and wood, and through glass in place of walls to break down barriers between the outside and inside. It would have a hearth at the center and would be horizontal and close to the earth. It would be free of historical styles and would be open and spacious, creating what Wright called the architecture of democracy.

As a result of these projects, Montana, a state not generally associated with Wright, has three standing Wright buildings to this day, representing two of the architect's phases, or sub-styles, as his modernist grammar evolved.[2]

THE BITTERROOT PROJECTS[3]

COMO ORCHARD

Wright's original mission in coming to Montana was to design the proposed "Como Orchard Summer Colony" near Darby for a local development company attempting to take advantage of an "apple boom" already under way in the Bitterroot Valley. The Bitterroot projects are associated with broader irrigation and financial speculation schemes, supported by a national enthusiasm for apple growing and the economic confidence that came with railroad building and social aspirations embedded in high-end Western tourism that took off at the end of the nineteenth century.[4] The Bitterroot apple boom resulted, in particular, from railroad expansion in Montana between 1883 and 1887, including a branch line from Missoula down the length of the Bitterroot Valley to Darby. This made the transport of agricultural produce from the valley possible at a time when developers were moving into the area and crop and livestock production was increasing to meet the needs of a growing valley population engaged in mining and timber operations. One of the developers was copper baron Marcus Daly, who started an irrigation canal north from Lake Como in 1887 to reclaim fertile benchland areas near Hamilton. Growers in the valley harvested alfalfa, oats, corn, barley, sugar beets, and other crops. But apples seemed to offer the best potential since fruit shipping was being accelerated in the U.S. at this time. Things really started to take off around 1906, with the construction of a large canal designed to irrigate 20,000 acres of Bitterroot Valley benchlands.[5] Thousands of acres of newly irrigable lands in the Bitterroot were purchased by newcomers, and numerous subdivisions were created, each with a golf course and inn. Since water was the key to development, municipal bonds were sold to residents and investors in 1908, creating the Bitter Root Irrigation District. The developers placed ads in eastern and midwestern newspapers, touting great profits that could be made by investors purchasing ten-acre apple orchard plots. Trainloads of potential investors began to arrive in Stevensville, Hamilton, and Darby.

The Como Orchard Summer Colony, one of the new Valley

Existing part of the "Big Ditch" irrigation canal system near Alpine Meadows Ranch, formerly Como Orchard Summer Colony. Photograph by Kathryn Hampton. Courtesy of Montana State Historic Preservation Office.

subdivisions, was the brainchild of Montana developer Samuel Dinsmore, who took over from Marcus Daly. Dinsmore was inspired by railroad expansion and hoped to follow on the success of apple orchards in Washington state's Yakima Valley and Hood River. He formed an irrigation company to start work on a necessary canal, but when he could not obtain local financing, he went out of state, enlisting Chicago developer W. I. Moody, who visited the valley in 1905 and invested heavily in the project, engaging in it full time. Moody's associate, Frederick Nichols, was put in charge of the project and began buying the land, laying out the canal, and enticing other capitalists to invest. Dinsmore's small irrigation company, bolstered by Moody's capitalization and participation, changed its name to the Bitter Root Valley Irrigation Company, BRVICo.[6]

What resulted was an early twentieth-century experiment in town planning. The Chicago developers had the land logged and began to dig a large irrigation canal, a fifty-six-mile "Big Ditch," that would connect two projects, the Como Orchard project and an envisioned second project, "Bitter Root Town," to follow farther north, near Stevensville. Both projects were under the control of BRVICo.

The original investors in the Como Orchard project were primarily University of Chicago professors, most of whom bought ten-acre lots at $400 per acre. They would build a cabin on their ten acres, choosing from plans offered by the company. In corporate brochures, Wright was not mentioned by name. The company would help take care of the apple trees, and in five years, when they started bearing fruit, the company would market the product for ten percent of the profit. The professors and their families could enjoy summers in Montana and reap income on the side.

It is believed that Frank Lloyd Wright was first contacted in Chicago by Nichols and Moody in December 1908 or January 1909 and invited to participate as the irrigation company's architect. He was asked to design the master plan for the initial Como Orchard project, called the "University Heights" subdivision, to include a central clubhouse, land office building, and fifty-one cottages. After surveying the site at Darby, Wright returned to his office in Oak Park, Illinois, and came up with an overall plan, dated April 1909, for University Heights.

Wright and his staff completed forty drawings: eight sheets of drawings for the cabins and three sheets for the clubhouse. There

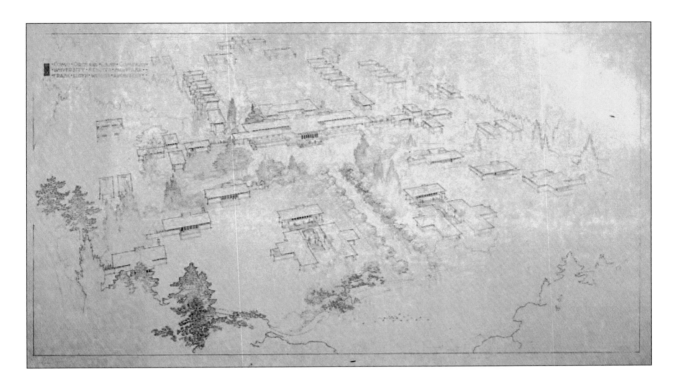

were three basic cabin designs, with several variations, consisting of one to four rooms, each having a rustic feel. The larger cabins were arranged symmetrically around a long central axis consisting of clubhouse, gardens, meadows, and pools. They would stand in front of the clubhouse. The smaller cabins were envisioned for the area behind the clubhouse. They would have no kitchens, and their owners would eat in the clubhouse.

The 213-foot-long clubhouse, the central lodge, was a two-story affair, on a cruciform pattern, with a two-story central lounge, three fieldstone fireplaces, and a planned long bank of tall windows overlooking the Sapphire Mountains. Two dining rooms extended outward from a central lounge on the first floor. Eighteen guest rooms were on the second floor and could be rented by visiting professors and potential investors looking over the project.

The cabins and clubhouse had the usual Prairie Style hallmarks: They were low and horizontal in appearance, with dark brown–stained board-and-batten siding, a cross-axial floor plan, spreading hipped roofs, overhanging eaves, bands of windows, broad chimneys, and natural fieldstone fireplaces.[7] The designs were clean and simple, like Japanese architecture, "organic," with no cluttering, employing the colors of nature and blending the buildings with the landscape.

Aerial view of Como Orchard Summer Colony complex, Darby, Montana, showing clubhouse and cabins as envisioned. Wright, Frank Lloyd (1867-1959) © ARS, NY. ©The Frank Lloyd Wright Fdn, AZ / Art Resource, NY. The Frank Lloyd Wright Foundation, Scottsdale, Arizona, U.S.A. (ART430571)

Side elevation, Como Orchard cabin. Wright, Frank Lloyd (1867-1959) © ARS, NY. ©The Frank Lloyd Wright Fdn, AZ / Art Resource, NY. The Frank Lloyd Wright Foundation, Scottsdale, Arizona, U.S.A. (ART430570)

Front elevation, Como Orchard Clubhouse. Wright, Frank Lloyd (1867-1959) © ARS, NY. ©The Frank Lloyd Wright Fdn, AZ / Art Resource, NY. The Frank Lloyd Wright Foundation, Scottsdale, Arizona, U.S.A. (ART430569). From 1910 Wasmuth Portfolio.

Wright broke down barriers between the inside and outside of the buildings through extensive utilization of glass, and the use of the same natural materials for the interior and exterior.

Wright's modernist grammar was functional, relying on structure and building materials in their natural state to provide design, with no tacked-on ornament. Window fenestration was one of the few sources of decoration in Wright's buildings, through the use of decorative wooden frames. The rest of the building's design was provided by its geometric shape, natural building materials, and engineering. Flat surfaces and straight lines predominated.

Construction on the clubhouse began on May 1, 1909, and shortly thereafter work began on the cabins.[8] By March 1910, the builders had erected the central clubhouse; a two-room smaller cottage converted into a land office; five three-bedroom cottages,

each 1,800 square feet; and six one-room cabins. Local contractors did the construction, working for BRVICo from Wright's plans, theoretically under the supervision of Wrights' Chicago-based assistants, Marion Mahoney and William Drummond.[9]

Although the structures conformed to Wright's plans, none was done exactly according to Wright's specifications. Wright did not return to supervise construction, nor is there any evidence that any of his office staff were involved. The actual structures were adapted from his original drawings by local craftsmen.[10] The Como Orchard plans, including clubhouse and cottages, were included in Wright's famous 1910 *Wasmuth Portfolio*, a volume of his major Prairie Style works up to that time, prepared for a major exhibit in Germany. These drawings, along with Wright's original plans, dated May 18, 1909, show clearly that deviations from Wright's drawings occurred during construction.

On the clubhouse, the second-floor balconies on each side of the lounge were removed, the flower boxes and wooden piers adding vertical elements to the facade were eliminated, and the continuous wrap-around band of windows was changed on the top floor. Horizontal battens were terminated by vertical trim at the

The Como Orchard Clubhouse shortly after construction. Photographer unknown. Courtesy of Montana Historical Society Photograph Archives.

The Como Orchard Land Office cabin as renovated. Photograph by Mary Greenfield. Courtesy of Montana State Historic Preservation Office.

The single remaining Como Orchard three-bedroom cottage. Photograph by Kathryn Hampton. Courtesy of the Montana State Historic Preservation Office.

corners rather than allowed to wrap around.[11] On the cabins, the plans were generally followed, but there were no extended exterior walls. Casement windows became sash windows, and the living room and porch were extended. The smaller, one-room land office had a second room added.[12] Still, the basic Wright details remain, including the use of hipped overhanging roofs, wide eaves, board-and-batten siding, and strip windows on the outside and, on the interior, the use of partitions and glass doors in place of walls, central stone fireplaces, built-in cabinets, mullion windows, and beamed ceilings. It should be noted that the dark-stained horizontal board-and-batten siding and some of the outside mullion pattern windows on the larger cottage have been

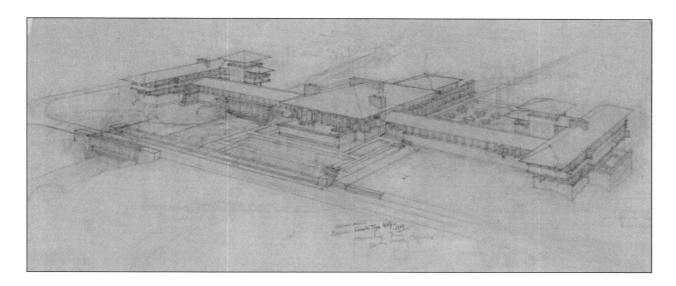

covered over by dark-stained vertical wooden plank siding and strip storm windows. But the original design has been maintained, and the mullion pattern windows remain on the interior window walls. The small cabin has been improved and the interior and exterior restored. It retains the horizontal board-and-batten siding on the exterior.[13]

The Como clubhouse and cabins were designed with a somewhat more rustic feel than Wright's larger, more elegant and detailed Prairie Style mansions in Chicago, Springfield, Grand Rapids, and Buffalo. The Montana cottages were inexpensive summer housing and were built more cheaply, having the rugged look of rough-hewn fibrous wood. They had no central heating and used pine blocks instead of concrete foundations. They belong to a "rustic" Prairie sub-genre termed "lake" or "forest" homes and cabins built first around the Great Lakes. They have the basic Prairie grammar, but are small, a bit over 1,500 square feet, light wood-framed structures, usually single story, devoid of art glass and built of brown-stained board-and-batten wood or lapped shingle siding, rather than brick and plaster.[14] The *Wasmuth Portfolio* described the Como Orchard project as "an arrangement of simple wooden cabins with a simple clubhouse."[15]

Other Wright clubhouse "rustics," comparable to the Como Orchard structures and Bitter Root Inn, include the 1902 Yahara Boathouse design for Madison, Wisconsin; the 1901 River Forest Tennis and 1904 River Forest Golf Clubs in Chicago; and the 1909 Estes Park Horseshoe Inn in Colorado. Other rustic cabins include the 1902 Gerts and 1909 Gale summer lakeside houses at Whitehall,

Architectural drawing, Horseshoe Inn, Estes Park, Colorado. Wright, Frank Lloyd (1867–1959) © ARS, NY. ©The Frank Lloyd Wright Fdn, AZ / Art Resource, NY. The Frank Lloyd Wright Foundation, Scottsdale, Arizona, U.S.A. (ART430565)

Walter S. Gerts Summer Cottage, Whitehall, Michigan. Wright, Frank Lloyd (1867–1959) © ARS, NY. ©The Frank Lloyd Wright Fdn, AZ / Art Resource, NY. The Frank Lloyd Wright Foundation, Scottsdale, Arizona, U.S.A. (ART430564)

Interior view of the last Como Orchard three-bedroom cottage, from living room looking out to sun porch. Photograph by Mary Greenfield. Courtesy of Montana State Historic Preservation Office.

Michigan; and the 1902 Spencer and Willis houses on Lake Delevan, Wisconsin.[16]

Like Como Orchard, the Delevan Lake project, although including only five houses, was designed by a Chicago developer as a summer retreat for wealthy Chicagoans. The Gerts cottage in Michigan is particularly close to the design of the larger Como three-bedroom cottages, with a similar floor plan of bedrooms and kitchen coming off the living room, and porch making a T-plan. It is very close in style as well, a single-story board-and-batten structure of rectangular plan, using rough-hewn dark-stained boards, with central stone fireplace, strip windows, and hipped roof.[17]

BITTER ROOT TOWN

Shortly after completing the design for Como Orchard, Wright was enlisted by W. I. Moody to do a second, more ambitious project in the Bitterroot Valley, to lay out a new "Town of Bitter Root," located six miles northeast of Stevensville, at the intersection of Eastside Highway and Three Mile Road, in the "Sunnyside" area.

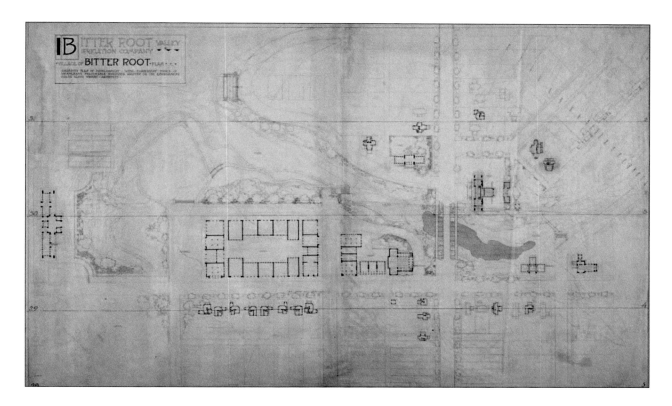

Whereas Como Orchard was a mountain retreat, this was to be more grandiose. "Bitter Root Town" was intended to be an attractive rural mountain community, an entire town with up to one thousand inhabitants living among 15,000 acres of apple orchards. It would be significant as one of Wright's earliest attempts at city planning.

Wright designed the town between April and October 1909, immediately after completing his plans for Como Orchard. In his plans for Bitter Root Town, he put together fifty-four buildings, to be built in a wide, flat valley, on a geometric grid of thirteen square blocks, each a quadrangle of four houses built around a central courtyard. This "quadruple block plan" first appeared in his February 1908 *Ladies Home Journal* article.[18] A depressed rail line would run under walkways and streets, creating a two-level transportation system. The central part of town would include a park-like mall, with residences radiating out from it into the pine forest. An opera house in the center of town would be the heart of city life. The railroad station would be located on the western edge of town. Everything was arranged functionally. Office blocks facing the central square would contain town services, a post office, fire house, telegraph office, real estate office, and bank. On the periphery of the grid

Aerial sketch of Bitter Root Town, as originally envisioned, Stevensville, Montana. Wright, Frank Lloyd (1867-1959) © ARS, NY. ©The Frank Lloyd Wright Fdn, AZ / Art Resource, NY. The Frank Lloyd Wright Foundation, Scottsdale, Arizona, U.S.A. (ART430568)

The Bitter Root Inn, ca. 1910.
Photographs by John J. Maloney.
Courtesy of the Montana Historical
Society Photograph Archives.

would be cultural activities: a theater with a fountain, a cultural
center, school, museum, library, and city administration building. To
the east would be the spacious Bitter Root Inn and a hospital, and to
the northeast would be suburban housing.[19]

The only structure actually built, however, was the Bitter
Root Inn, completed in October 1910 and opened in February 1911,

although some work had begun on a golf course, several houses, a store, and a dentist office. Potential visitors from the East were brought in by the trainload and entertained at the inn, but BRVICo soon realized that the plan was too grandiose and asked Wright to design a smaller village plan and buildings for the city center. The second plan was totally different, with only a few public buildings.[20] Wright referred to this project only twice in later discussions. In his 1932 *Autobiography*, he wrote simply that he was involved in it with no elaboration. In 1942 recollections, recorded by art historian Henry Russell Hitchcock, Wright said, "There were two projects for a town of Bitter Root on much the same site, prepared earlier for the irrigation company." Hitchcock noted, "His memory was hazy on these projects."[21]

The Bitter Root Inn turned out to be a much scaled-down version of the Como Orchard Clubhouse, with dining and reception rooms, offices on the lower floors, and guest rooms upstairs. It was a 126-foot-long board-and-batten, two-story structure, sweeping, with low gabled, rather than hipped, overhanging roof, and specially patterned banks of windows. It was also T-shaped, with a long full-length veranda. Pillars and pedestals added vertical elements. There were fewer deviations from Wright's plans.[22] Like the Como Orchard Clubhouse, the Bitter Root Inn fit in with the other "rustic" resort buildings. BRVICo carpenters apparently built both buildings. Based on photographs, it appears that the Bitter Root Inn was built with somewhat greater attention to Wright's plans than the Como Orchard Clubhouse.

Various Bitter Root Town house plans created by Wright were available at the company office. They were square designs of board and batten, similar to those at Como Orchard, except many were two story and some had gabled roofs. There is an ongoing debate whether any were actually constructed, as BRVICo records were destroyed in a 1924 fire that consumed the Bitter Root Inn. The Stevensville Historical Society cites local claims that, in addition to the Bitter Root Inn, BRVICo built four residences nearby, two of which still stand. This is supported by Cheryl Linduska's article in a *Ravalli Republican* newspaper supplement, noting that "two craftsman style homes on the East Side Highway near the former site of the Bitter Root Inn were possibly built from Bitter

Bitter Root Town, a typical house floor plan and a front elevation drawing. Wright, Frank Lloyd (1867–1959) © ARS, NY. ©The Frank Lloyd Wright Fdn, AZ / Art Resource, NY. The Frank Lloyd Wright Foundation, Scottsdale, Arizona, U.S.A. (ART430566 and ART430567)

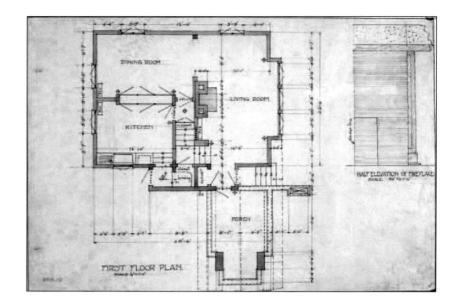

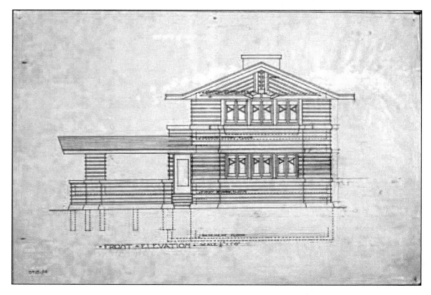

Root Town cabin plans supplied by Wright's office." Donald Leslie Johnson, however, claims to have investigated the two houses in question and confirmed that they were not Wright houses. He says Mrs. Moody, the owner of the Bitter Root Inn property plus one of the two houses in question, checked the county building records and found that the two houses were built by a competent bungalow designer in 1912. A third Craftsman house in question, on the East Side Highway, was probably built after 1918.[23] You can see from the accompanying photographs that the houses are of Craftsman design and bear similarities to Wright's Prairie Style

One of the two still standing 1912 Craftsman-style houses on the Eastside Highway near the Bitter Root Town location. Determined not to be a Frank Lloyd Wright design. Photograph courtesy of John Driscoll.

architectural grammar, including the use of board-and-batten siding (although vertical in this case), hip roofs, central fireplaces, broad roof overhangs, dark-stained oak trims, muntin-framed window patterns, built-in furniture, and interior stringcourse moldings. However, these features were also prevalent in Arts and Crafts–influenced, non-Wright Bungalow and Craftsman houses of the era. Other houses in nearby Hamilton, Montana, were rumored to have been designed by Wright during his 1909 visit to the city, including one by Missoula architect Perry Endsley, who claimed that he persuaded Wright during his stay to design a house for his daughter on South Third Street. Donald Leslie Johnson concluded that there is no evidence to support this.[24]

The Endsley House has numerous Wright influences (hipped, pagoda-styled, layered roofs with overhangs, horizontal overall design, layered shingle siding, and central fireplace), but also some deviations from the Prairie Style. The house includes a porch and basement, two elements that Wright did not use, and it also has some of what Wright called "holes punched in walls," or individual windows on the facade, rather than relying strictly on Wright's preferred ribbons of windows, joined together. Johnson feels that someone tried to emulate Wright's style, but missed the proportions, details, and fenestration.[25]

A 1918 Craftsman-style house on the Eastside Highway near the location of Bitter Root Town. Determined not to be a Frank Lloyd Wright design. Photograph courtesy of John Driscoll.

The Endsley House on South Third Street, Hamilton, Montana. Similar to Frederick Nichols House in Flossmoor, Illinois. Photograph courtesy of John Driscoll.

FAILURE IN THE BITTERROOT

Unfortunately, the Bitterroot projects ended in failure. The reason is not entirely clear. The apple boom was short-lived. In 1913, a blight hit the Bitterroot Valley, wiping out much of the crop. High shipping costs and bad weather were apparently contributing factors, and according to one local resident interviewed later, soil conditions may not have been good for the McIntosh red apples, which "never ripened into prosperity."[26] The Big Ditch irrigation canal could barely deliver sufficient water, and expensive wooden flumes and siphons required constant upkeep.[27] BRVICo went bankrupt in 1916 when the banks foreclosed. Disappointing returns on apples apparently led investors to stop paying their taxes and abandon their plots.[28] A Montana Bureau of Reclamation report claims that the irrigation canals and ditches suffered excessive leakage and breaks from the beginning.[29] There were numerous lawsuits.

Even before the blight, however, there had not been a lot of success in attracting potential investors, even though the company brought out trainloads of academics for stays in the Como clubhouse.[30] Moody and Nichols quit the venture early on, in April 1910, before all the orchards were planted or buildings completed,[31] just as the "Big Ditch" was being finished. This was still three years before the blight hit.

New owners (the DuPont Company) purchased the Como Orchard project in 1923 and renamed it the McIntosh and Morello Orchards. Apples were phased out between 1924 and 1930, and the owners brought in sheep and cattle. In 1937, local rancher Joe Abbey of Darby, who had been sheep manager for McIntosh and Morello, bought out DuPont's interest and raised sheep and cattle. After years of disuse, all but two of the eleven original cottages were torn down in the late 1930s. The empty clubhouse was altered and whitewashed, used as a hall to house workers and store hog feed, and finally turned into a packing hall. In a state of decay, it was finally dismantled in 1945, after the property was sold by Abbey to another rancher. The boards were used to build a barn.[32] Fortunately, one larger cottage and the smaller cottage that served as a land office were able to survive. The larger cottage is still in good shape, in its original form, and is now rented out on a weekly basis to vacationers as part of the new Alpine Meadows Ranch. The land office was altered considerably, but still has Wright touches and stands as part of the original complex.

The nearby "Bitter Root Town," which had only one building, the Bitter Root Inn, also floundered when the bank foreclosed in 1916, halting all development. As with Como Orchard, it never found its footing. The inn, which opened in 1911, had no lodgers and was used for classrooms for a while, then as a dance hall. On July 28, 1924, it burned to the ground.

THE MYSTERY REGARDING WRIGHT'S ROLE

According to Wright historian Grant Carpenter Manson, Como Orchard became an "office tragedy" for the Wright firm. Its failure damaged not only the Chicago professors who financed the project, but also Wright himself, who had possibly put some of his scanty capital, plus untold hours of time and thought, into the venture. It became one of Wright's "ill starred projects," an uncompleted Montana utopia.[33]

There are a lot of unanswered questions and some mystery about the projects' failure and whether Wright pulled out early. The Bitterroot projects coincided with a time of personal crisis for Wright, a period, from 1909 to 1910, when he was in the midst of an affair with Mamah Cheney, the wife of a Chicago neighbor for whom he had built a house in 1902. Wright asked his wife for a divorce only five months before his trip to Montana. Eight months after his visit to Montana, in October 1909, Wright and his mistress departed for a year in Europe, leaving behind her husband and two children and Wright's wife and their six children. It was during these eight troubled months that Wright was designing the Bitterroot projects. And despite claims that his assistants, Marion Mahoney and Walter Burley Griffin, supervised construction at Como Orchard and Bitter Root Town after he left for Europe, there is no evidence that they actually did. Wright later said that the projects were constructed "without supervision."[34]

Wright may have lost the Como Orchard commission before he left for Europe, or more likely, he had completed his work. The possibility that Wright was hired only as the "architect" for the Irrigation Company may be borne out by local newspaper advertisements for orchard cottages at this time, saying "any competent carpenter or builder, on the basis of the plans in the hands of the company, can meet the (construction) requirements, building in harmony of the general architectural ideal."[35] BRVICo obviously felt local talent was sufficient to use Wright's plans.[36]

There may be a lot of unanswered questions regarding Wright's role, but the real reason for the failure of the uncompleted Bitterroot enterprise was the failure of the project itself, not of Wright's buildings. The cause of BRVICo's partial downfall was the lack of Chicago investors and the failure of the apple boom on which they depended. What we don't know is whether Wright's designated assistants communicated with BRVICo regarding construction during his absence. Was Wright disappointed, or was he merely a contract architect hired to come up with initial plans? Did he lose his own money on the project?

Unfortunately, there is a lack of records. Henry Russell Hitchcock, in his massive review of Wright papers and projects, lamented that it would have been of interest if there had been more documents than just the Como Orchard plans about the Bitterroot projects in the Taliesin archives. Grant Manson supported this, noting that the lack of records could be attributed to the Taliesin fire of 1914 and to the office "debacle of 1909–10."[37] More recent researchers have also been unable to turn up anything, either at Taliesin or in the Bitterroot. Delwan Ludwig, researching in 1982, said "information was scarce." Courtney Graham Donnell, in her 1974 Montana State University thesis, concluded that much work could still be done to clarify Wright's Bitterroot projects. Donald Leslie Johnson, who reviewed the Frank Lloyd Wright Taliesin archives in 1987, claimed the archives do not contain relevant material of the period, that neither Taliesin nor BRVICo records contain correspondence prior to 1913.[38]

LASTING SIGNIFICANCE

Montana is fortunate in that the Bitterroot projects left the state with two Frank Lloyd Wright buildings: two early Wright "rustic" Prairie Houses, which are two of the few Prairie Houses ever built west of the Mississippi River. We have been left with a Wright legacy. Bitterroot resident Bessie Monroe, who lived through the apple "boom and bust," put it best in a 1970s newspaper interview, saying that "Wright went home to Illinois sadder but wiser, but he left behind the imprint of his genius."[39]

We can thank Alpine Meadows Ranch proprietor Charles Rowland, the current owner of the Como Orchard site, for his long-term interest in Frank Lloyd Wright and for maintaining Wright's memory in Montana. He has preserved the two remaining Wright cottages, now listed on the National Register of Historic Places, and continues to promote Wrightian principles, as seen also in the

The remaining Como Orchard three-bedroom cottage, north elevation, looking south. Photograph by Mary Greenfield. Courtesy of Montana State Historic Preservation Office.

resort's new Cider House. Montana could probably make more of the fact that it has two Wright buildings in the Bitterroot. Moreover, the original Como Orchard Type C cottage is one of only a handful of existing Frank Lloyd Wright buildings, out of 475 standing, that can be rented in the United States—where visitors can actually stay overnight. The others include the Biltmore Hotel in Phoenix, Arizona; Park Hotel in Mason City, Iowa; Price Tower in Bartlesville, Oklahoma; and Seth Peterson Cottage in Lake Delton, Wisconsin.

The Bitterroot projects, although almost entirely gone, remain significant parts of Wright's architectural legacy, joining the ranks of other major "Lost Wright" works, now gone but not forgotten. These include the 1912 Francis Little House in Minnesota, the 1903 Larkin Administration Building in Buffalo, the 1914 Midway Gardens in Chicago, and Tokyo's 1916 Imperial Hotel. All were Wright landmarks in architectural modernism. Como Orchard and Bitter Root Town have particular significance, along with the Stewart house in Montecito, California, as Wright's first forays into the West.[40] They mark a dividing line between Wright's first (Pre-Prairie and Prairie

House) career and his second (Japan, California, Arizona) career.

The Bitterroot projects occupy a significant place in architectural modernism through their inclusion in the *Wasmuth Portfolio*, a collection of Wright's early works with his introduction, published in 1911, which greatly influenced European modernists like Mies van der Rohe, Peter Behrens, and Le Corbusier. The *Portfolio* contains four plates of illustrations on Como Orchard, an honor shared with only three other of the seventy-two Frank Lloyd Wright projects displayed, those being the renowned Coonley and Dana Houses and Unity Temple, all in Illinois. This would also seem to indicate that Wright felt Como Orchard was one of his most important architectural works,[41] one of his better designs.

The Bitterroot experiments are important landmarks for town planning in America. Wright had dabbled with community planning prior to 1910, but the Bitterroot plans were his most ambitious schemes. Como Orchard and Bitter Root Town represent Wright's version of community, an idea he would continue to develop. His idea was to get people out of the larger cities, which he called man killers. He wanted to create a new way of living for mankind, more in tune with nature, in tune with man's inner nature. Wright was interested in using architecture to change man by putting him in touch with his roots. He would accomplish this by building "organic" architecture that blended in with the land it was built on.

His idea was to blend suburban and agrarian lifestyles, getting Chicago professors and their families out of the big city in the summers, putting them in nature in the Bitterroot, and giving them some outdoor activity in the process, tending their orchards. They would live and work together, communal but independent, each with his own house and a ten-acre plot of land with apple trees. They would be encouraged to dine together in the clubhouse, as most of the cabins had no kitchens.

Como Orchard was a smaller, more resort-like scheme, what Wright referred to as a "community of like minded individuals," in this case professors who admired nature, united together in a community. This concept was employed later by Wright on a more suburban basis at Parkwyn Village in Kalamazoo, Michigan, for employees of Upjohn Pharmaceuticals, and at Lake Delevan, Wisconsin, where Chicago professionals created their own community. But these models were not as communal as Como Orchard and did not have the agricultural component.

Bitter Root Town would take the Como Orchard plan to a larger level, with residents living together in a community of one thousand. But it would be a town for everyone, with different categories of housing, some modest, some larger, all with connected plots for orchards. The life of the village would be the central meeting house where concerts would be held and the community could enjoy culture. At the same time, residents lived close to the soil. They could help finance their lives through what they grew.

Bitter Root Town, despite its size and downtown buildings, was a planned community, a village for those who appreciated Wright's organic, semi-agrarian lifestyle, off the grid and self-sustaining. Wright would enhance this concept in his seminal Broadacre City plan of 1935, creating a village of houses with one-acre gardens that the owners maintained, with a central market in the village square where they could sell their produce. Never built, Broadacre was to be a city combining farm and factory, roadside and farmers' markets, leisure places for culture, with organized recreational and cultural activities to build a relationship between culture and nature. Bitter Root Town and Como Orchard's "University Heights" were its antecedents.

These projects are also significant as early experiments in low-cost housing. The cottages were built for this purpose, without trim and decoration, for summer living only, and they were much more modest in size than the usual Prairie Houses. They were standardized, with off-the-shelf plans. Other examples of Wright's low-cost housing experiments include the 1895 Francisco and 1901 Lexington Apartments in Chicago, grouped around courtyards; the 1911–17 American Ready Cut System of prefabricated houses in Milwaukee; the 1939 Sun Top houses in Ardmore, Pennsylvania; his 1950s Erdman Pre-fabricateds; and the concrete block, self-built "Usonian Automatics." Wright scholars Hildebrand and Bosworth see this modest piece in Montana within the corpus of Wright's work as perhaps the first tentative step toward modular planning that prevailed in the textile block houses of the 1920s and in the post–World War II Usonians.[42]

WHITEFISH, MONTANA: THE LOCKRIDGE CLINIC

The Whitefish clinic, begun in 1961, two years after Wright's death, and completed in 1963, was one of a handful of Usonian medical buildings that Wright created toward the end of his career. The clinic functioned for a year until Dr. T. L. Lockridge passed away, and then was taken over by First State Bank, which made some renovations. It was finally purchased in 2002 by the Morrison and Frampton Law Firm, which has maintained the building well and proudly displays the building's Wrightian provenance on a large sign out front. A red square ceramic tile with Wright's signature is embedded in the original brickwork near the entrance, Wright's personal imprimatur, only given to buildings that met with his personal approval. The law firm has made a few minor renovations, but managed to keep the building true to Wright's original design. Architectural historian William Allin Storrer paid tribute to the Morrison and Frampton firm for maintaining and opening the building to visitors. Like Charles Rowland in the Bitterroot, Morrison and Frampton have done historical preservation on their own in Whitefish.

The initial building design was done by Wright, with John Howe, his chief draftsman, doing the preliminary designs. Construction was not supervised by Taliesin Associated Architects, but was "of the highest order," completed by a skilled carpenter in Whitefish who

The First State Bank, formerly Lockridge Clinic, Whitefish, Montana. Wright, Frank Lloyd (1867-1959) © ARS, NY. ©The Frank Lloyd Wright Fdn, AZ / Art Resource, NY. The Frank Lloyd Wright Foundation, Scottsdale, Arizona, U.S.A. (ART430572)

Interior, First State Bank, formerly Lockridge Clinic, Whitefish, Montana. Wright, Frank Lloyd (1867–1959) © ARS, NY. ©The Frank Lloyd Wright Fdn, AZ / Art Resource, NY. The Frank Lloyd Wright Foundation, Scottsdale, Arizona, U.S.A. (ART430573).

visited Taliesin to familiarize himself with Wright's methods.[43]

The 128-foot-long, 5,000-square-foot clinic is a typical Wrightian design: single story, horizontal, with an "I" or "on-line" floor plan. The exterior is wood and glass: a combination of bricks of a variegated orange-tan hue, and a 64-foot bank of floor-to-ceiling windows, framed with Philippine mahogany trim painted Cherokee Red, Wright's favorite color. To emphasize the building's horizontal thrust, Wright had the mortar raked a half inch deep on the horizontal joints, while those on the vertical were left flush. Decoration on the facade was provided by a white concrete fascia in a "reverse curve." This contrasts with the warm wood and brick tones. The building's highest element is a lapped dark-stained board parapet, formerly a rooftop planter.[44]

Inside, the atmosphere, by design, is more reminiscent of a domestic living room than a doctor's office. Wright used warm colors and natural materials to impart a sense of serenity and comfort. A massive brick fireplace, the centerpiece of Wright's designs since his earliest commissions, served as the focal point of the waiting room, with two built-in curved banquettes flanking the fireplace to form an inglenook. Specially designed low tables for children were set near the windows. The unobtrusive reception desk adds to this illusion of a normal living room in a home rather than a clinic. Natural light filtered in through a double clerestory window above the front wall that faced west.[45]

Examination rooms, nurses' quarters, and an x-ray unit were placed on either side of the waiting area, and skylights brought light into the working areas. Wright engineered a pleasing view for the patients by including plans for a landscaped garden filled with low bushes and perennials.[46]

Overall, the building has the typical grammar of Wright's last, modernist or Usonian phase, begun in 1936, but dominating his work after World War II. The Usonians were smaller, single-story designs. They were very horizontal, with low-pitched or flat roofs and broad overhanging eaves, rows of mullion-patterned windows, board-and-batten and brick walls, glossy concrete floors, plywood furniture, and large wood-framed windows and doors opening up the entire rear vista. The Usonians were made of standardized materials, usually cypress and Philippine mahogany, and there was always a hearth, or fireplace, in the center. Clerestory windows, high up, coaxed in extra light.[47] The Lockridge Clinic conformed to this phase.

Usonians like the Lockridge Clinic reflected Wright's desire to create more modest, less expensive homes or offices to meet the need for a growing suburban middle class after World War II, using concrete, plywood, and built-in furniture to get rid of the complications in construction seen in his previous Prairie-era art glass windows, overhanging hip roofs, and interior trim. This would eliminate expensive labor. Wright would create a sense of spaciousness and simplicity. He would combine simple shapes and warm, natural materials. There would be little ornament, less than ever before in his houses.

But the Usonians, like the Lockridge Clinic, still fit in with Wright's basic principles, which changed forms with the times and locales, but stayed the same from 1901 to 1959. There was always the emphasis on simplicity, using flat geometric planes. There would be little, if any, added-on ornament or decoration like painted walls, shutters, and dormers. The building's structure and building materials would provide decoration—"form following function," as we saw in the earlier Bitterroot designs. This applies both to the Prairie buildings with board-and-batten and overhanging roofs and muntin-framed windows at Darby and Stevensville in 1909 and to the tinted brick and concrete fascia at Whitefish fifty years later.

THE LOCKRIDGE CLINIC IN THE CONTEXT OF WRIGHT'S WORK

Montana is testimony to the longevity of Frank Lloyd Wright's career. The Bitterroot projects were initiated in 1909, with Model T cars in the drive. Lockridge Clinic was initiated in 1958, half a century later, with passenger jets flying overhead.

Wright had changed a lot in the fifty years between Bitterroot and Whitefish. He was forty-one in 1908, married to his first wife, Catherine, his practice based in Chicago, and he was not yet well known. Fame would come first in Europe, with his travels to Berlin and publication of his works in the *Wasmuth Portfolio*. His European success would gain him recognition in America and lead to a major commission in Japan, the Imperial Hotel. Its survival of the terrible earthquake that leveled Tokyo in 1923 added to his name. Later, in 1935, his Fallingwater House in Pennsylvania, built over a waterfall, would occupy the covers of numerous magazines, giving him lasting fame.

By the time Wright got involved again in Montana, in 1958, he would have gone through fifty years and through four phases in his career, each distinct, as his style changed to fit his new locales, first the well-known Prairie Style that lasted until 1910; and then the pre-Columbian "Textile Block" houses of patterned concrete blocks in Los Angeles in the early twenties with his new wife, Miriam Noel. Then he made the move to a more streamlined and plastic look, sometimes with curves, similar to the European International Modern style, but with texture and nature added and more glass and poured concrete; this was the 1935–38 period of Fallingwater, the Johnson Wax Administration Building, and Taliesin West. In 1938, at the height of this new phase, Wright was seventy-one, but still healthy and vigorous. He was married to Olgivanna, his fourth and final wife, who helped him to establish a Taliesin Fellowship of young apprentices, write his autobiography, and move to Arizona.

And finally, taking off after World War II, came the last phase (he hated the word "style") of his career, the Usonian. This included the first Jacobs House in Wisconsin (1936), the Pope-Leighy house in Virginia (1939), the Rosenbaum House in Alabama (1939), the Zimmerman House in New Hampshire, and the Walter House in Iowa (1950). In all, 140 Usonians were built.

Two other Usonian-style medical clinics are very similar to the Lockridge, with clerestory windows set above plate glass, floor-to-ceiling panes, and with multiple roof heights. The Meyers Clinic in Dayton (1956) has stacked rosewood roofs containing a chimney. The Kundert Clinic in San Luis Obispo (1955) has multiple (three) clerestories that are used to bring in light. Both are ophthalmology clinics, like the Lockridge.

In the mid-1950s, Wright began experimenting with the curve. Traditionally, his work had been straight line and rectilinear. Now, he began to use the circle in both structure and design. We see this in his "hemicycles," houses with curved facades to catch the sun as it traverses the sky. And we see other round buildings, the Guggenheim Museum in New York (1956), the Kalita Humphreys Theater in Dallas (1955), his Plan for Greater Baghdad (1957–58), the Marin County Civic Center in California (1957), the David Wright and Normal Lykes houses (1959) in Scottsdale, and the Grady Gammage Auditorium in Phoenix (1959). This circular phase is the final sub-genre of the last, "Usonian," period. Wright was, at the time, weaving architecture out of opposites, the circle and the square.[48]

As part of this sub-phase, Wright was beginning to use "reverse curves" for decoration. The "reverse curves" we see in the Lockridge Clinic fascia are also in the Annunciation Greek Orthodox Church windows in Wisconsin (1957) and in the decorative motif of the Grady Gammage Auditorium.

The Lockridge Clinic, although simple and unadorned, is one of Wright's finer works, the complete model of his Usonian ideal, reflecting geometry and the modern world's practical aesthetic. The Lockridge, like all Usonians, represents Wright's architecture of American democracy: open and spacious, and rejecting historical styles.

CONCLUSION

Wright always looked for beautiful settings for his works, and he certainly found the perfect locations under the Big Sky. He grew up in Wisconsin and did most of his work in the Midwest, until the 1920s. It is noteworthy that he chose Montana for one of his first forays outside his home region, building one of the first Prairie structures west of the Mississippi River in the Bitterroot. In the process, he chose Montana as the perfect place for his friends, Chicago professors and businessmen, to have summer cottages. Interestingly, one of his last projects was in Montana as well, in the clinic in the Flathead area for Dr. Lockridge.

Only three of Wright's Montana buildings remain, two cabins and the clinic. It is a shame that the Bitter Root Inn, and the Como Orchard Clubhouse, large works, like many of his grandiose projects, did not survive as times changed and nature took its toll, and that Bitter Root Town did not get off the ground. But this is not unusual, as many of Wrights projects have been lost over time. Their loss, however, points up the need for historic preservation. It would be nice to see these inns and cottages rebuilt, just as the Yahara Boathouse has recently been built in Buffalo, based on the 1902 plans.

Yet, these projects were not really lost, since they remain part of Wright's folklore, and part of the architectural modernism record, a record begun around 1900 in Chicago, Vienna, and Glasgow, with Wright at the forefront. The Montana works are included in the best studies on early Wright and discussed in great detail in Henry Russell Hitchcock's seminal study, *In the Nature of Materials*. They occupy a prominent place in the famous *Wasmuth Portfolio* of Wright's buildings, produced in Germany in 1911, a book that had a profound effect on LeCorbusier, Gropius, and Mies van der Rohe.

The surviving Wright buildings, at Alpine Meadows, and in Whitefish, continue to draw Wright scholars from around the world. As with the "lost" Midway Gardens in Chicago, the Larkin Building in Buffalo, and the Imperial Hotel in Tokyo, the Wrightian legacy survives in Montana. We had, and have, major, significant Wright projects, and we are favored in having architectural bookends, the Como Cabin C3 and the Lockridge Clinic, representing early and late Wright phases, showcasing his development as well as the evolution of modernism in the twentieth century. Wright's projects are important parts of Montana's modernist architectural history, which includes buildings by Cass Gilbert, Richard Neutra, and William Gray Purcell, among others. Fittingly, in 2012, both Wright Montana properties, in the Bitterroot and at Whitefish, were formally listed in the National Register of Historic Places.

NOTES

1   National Register of Historic Places Registration
     Form, University Heights Historic District/Lake Como
     Orchards; Alpine Meadows Ranch nomination (on file at
     Montana State Preservation Office [SHPO]), 12.

2   Email correspondence with Patty Dean, March 3, 2012,
     Montana Preservation Alliance.

3   For the history of the Bitterroot projects and the
     Montana apple boom, see Tina Marie Bell, *Bitter
     Root Project*, Montana Reclamation Project, Bureau
     of Reclamation, U.S. Department of Interior, 1998;
     Montana State Historic Preservation Office nomination
     of two Como Orchard cabins for the National Register
     of Historic Places, 2012; Courtney Graham, "Prairie
     School Town Planning, 1900–1915," Master's Thesis, New
     York University, 1974; Donald Leslie Johnson, "Frank
     Lloyd Wright's Architectural Projects in the Bitterroot
     Valley, 1909–10," *Montana The Magazine of Western
     History* (37), 1987; and Delton Ludwig, "Frank Lloyd
     Wright in the Bitterroot Valley of Montana," in *The
     Frank Lloyd Wright Newsletter* 5, 1982.

4   University Heights nomination, SHPO, 12.

5   Ibid.

6   Ibid., 16.

7   See full description of Wright touches in Dixie Legler,
     Frank Lloyd Wright: The Western Work (San Francisco:
     Chronicle Books, 1999), 15.

8   Ludwig, "Wright in the Bitterroot," 21.

9   Grant Hildebrand and Thomas Bosworth, "The Last
     Cottage of Wright's Como Orchards Project," *Journal
     of the Society of Architectural Historians* 41 (1982): 325.

10   University Heights nomination, SHPO, 20.

11   Ludwig, "Wright in the Bitterroot," 13.

12   Hildebrand and Bosworth, "The Last Cottage," 325–327.

13   These changes are listed in the University Heights
     nomination, SHPO.

14   William Allin Storrer, *The Frank Lloyd Wright Companion*
     (Chicago: University of Chicago Press, 1994), 128; Henry-
     Russell Hitchcock, in *In the Nature of Materials: The
     Buildings of Frank Lloyd Wright, 1887–1941* (New York: De
     Capo Press, 1975), 39–46, discusses the evolution of the
     Prairie Style, noting that Prairie Houses can be grouped
     by size and cost, materials, or even roof type, but with
     basic Wrightian precepts.

15   Ludwig notes this in "Wright in the Bitterroot," 7,
     referring to the 1910 *Wasmuth Portfolio*, plate 46.

16   In *In the Nature of Materials*, Hitchcock refers to these
     as "forest" houses.

17   Storrer, *The Wright Companion*, 75.

18   William Allin Storrer, *The Architecture of Frank Lloyd
     Wright: A Complete Catalog*, 2nd Edition (Cambridge:
     MIT Press, 1978), 148.

19   Legler, *The Western Work*,14–17.

20   Brooks Pfeiffer, *Frank Lloyd Wright Monographs, 1907–
     13* (Tokyo: APA Press, 1987), 167.

21   Quoted in Donald Leslie Johnson, "Further Notes on
     Frank Lloyd Wright in the Bitterroot Valley," Montana
     Historical Society Research Center, 5.

22   Ludwig, "Wright in the Bitterroot," 13.

23   Johnson, "Further Notes," 5–6.

24   Ibid.

25   Ibid.

26   Ibid., 6.

27   University Heights nomination, SHPO, 20.

28   Stevensville Historical Society, *Montana Genesis:
     History of the Stevensville Area of the Bitterroot Valley*
     (Missoula, MT: Mountain Press, 1971), 17.

29   Bell, *Bitter Root Project*, 7.

30   Grant Carpenter Manson, *Frank Lloyd Wright to 1910:
     The First Golden Age* (New York: Reinhold Publishing,
     1958), 202.

31   Johnson, "Further Notes," 15.

32   Ludwig, "Wright in the Bitterroot," 22.

33   Manson, *Frank Lloyd Wright to 1910*, 207.

34   Johnson, "Projects in the Bitterroot Valley," 18.

35   J. Nichols, *Western News*, May 1910.

36   Johnson, "Projects in the Bitterroot Valley," 18.

37   Manson, *Frank Lloyd Wright to 1910*, 217.

38   Johnson, "Further Notes," 14.

39   Ibid., 6.

40   Arthur Dyson, introduction to Legler, *The Western
     Work*, 9.

41   Johnson, "Projects in the Bitterroot Valley," 16.

42   See Hildebrand and Bosworth, "The Last Cottage," 327.

43   Legler, *The Western Work*, 106–109, quoted in pamphlet
     at Morrison and Frampton Law Firm (former Lockridge
     Medical Clinic building).

44   Ibid.

45   Ibid.

46   Ibid.

47   Donald W. Hofmann, *The Seven Ages of Frank Lloyd
     Wright* (Santa Barbara: Capra Press, 1993), 176.

48   Ibid., 158.

ABOUT THE AUTHOR

Randall LeCocq, a retired Foreign Service Officer, resides in Helena, Montana, where he serves on the Board of Directors of Drumlummon Institute, a nonprofit dedicated to the promotion of Montana arts and culture. Randy has taught and lectured on art history and literature in New Mexico and Montana. He completed his Masters of Liberal Studies at Georgetown University, where his thesis compared Frank Lloyd Wright to the early twentieth-century European modernists.

ALSO AVAILABLE FROM DRUMLUMMON INSTITUTE

(To purchase, visit our online store at: drumlummon.org/html/Online%20Store.htm)

"The Whole Country was . . . 'One Robe'"
The Little Shell Tribe's America
by Nicholas C. P. Vrooman

Lona Hanson: A Novel
by Thomas Savage (introduction by O. Alan Weltzien)

Old Friends & New
A Compact Disc
The Wilbur Rehmann Quintet

Splendid on a Large Scale
The Writings of Hans Peter Gyllembourg Koch,
Montana Territory, 1869–1874
Kim Allen Scott, editor

Coming Home
Drumlummon Views, Volume 3, No. 1 (Spring 2009)
A Special Issue Devoted to the Historic Built Environment
and Landscapes of Butte and Anaconda, Montana
Patty Dean, editor

Robert Harrison: The Architecture of Space
Essays by Rick Newby & Glen R. Brown

The Pass: A Novel
by Thomas Savage (introduction by O. Alan Weltzien)

Notes for a Novel: The Selected Poems of Frieda Fligelman
Alexandra Swaney & Rick Newby, editors

Food of Gods and Starvelings: The Selected Poems of
Grace Stone Coates
Lee Rostad & Rick Newby, editors

Grace Stone Coates: Her Life in Letters
by Lee Rostad

Grace Stone Coates: Honey Wine and Hunger Root
Lee Rostad, editor

Available only through Blurb.com
(search Blurb by title)

Long Lines of Dancing Letters:
The Japanese Drawings of Patricia Forsberg
Essay by Rick Newby

Drumlummon Views, Volume 2, No. 1 (Fall 2008)
[See http://drumlummon.org/html/DV_Jump-page.html
for all issues of **Drumlummon Views**
the online journal of Montana arts & culture]

Made in the USA
Middletown, DE
19 February 2016